Libertarian Rants

*A Critique of
Western Culture
from a
Libertarian Perspective*

MICHAEL SCHULTE

Libertarian Rants

*A Critique of
Western Culture
from a
Libertarian Perspective*

MICHAEL SCHULTE

PALMETTO
PUBLISHING
Charleston, SC
www.PalmettoPublishing.com

Hardcover ISBN: 979-8-8229-4910-2
Paperback ISBN: 979-8-8229-4534-0
eBook ISBN: 979-8-8229-4535-7

Front cover: Seurat, Georges (1881). A Man Leaning on a Parapet [Painting].

Metropolitan Museum of Art, New York, NY, United States.

https://www.metmuseum.org/art/collection/search/438 123 Public domain

Dedication

Dedicated to every person who, knowingly or unknowingly,
longs for a libertarian restoration of civilization
and the ultimate triumph of free markets, free speech,
property rights, and personal agency.

Contents

Dedication · v

Preface · ix

Warm-Up Rants · 1

Interlude – The Greeks Chime In · · · · · · · · · · · · · · · · · · · 21

Rants in the Main · 31

*Interlude – Twisted Nursery Rhyme*s · · · · · · · · · · · · · · · · 57

Rants For Change · 69

Acknowledgment · 96

About the Author · 97

Preface

Libertarian Rants is the result of my desire to influence culture. But how to do it? Talking with friends, family, and neighbors was no longer enough. Nor was voting or peaceful protest. And writing was not on my radar. I have always been an avid reader, but writing for publication came to me late in life.

My first foray into journalism came about with little planning. On a dare, I brought my resume to the local newspaper editor after hearing the paper was looking for writers. He did have freelance openings, but it wasn't for the serious, hard-hitting journalism that I envisioned. Truth be known, I had no experience writing hard-hitting stuff.

Furthermore, my small-town newspaper had no interest in that type of journalism. I was hired to write business feature articles. Grateful for the opportunity and having learned much about journalism thanks to a patient editor, I retained the desire to write about things that mattered more.

Later, poetry, especially limericks, became an avenue for me to express myself. Several of my friends and colleagues reminded me that limericks were only one type of poetry, strongly hinting that I should expand my repertoire. Quatrains, haiku, free verse, found poetry, and other forms of poetry became subjects of interest. Soon I was counting syllables, verifying meter, establishing rhyme, counting stanzas, and more. Eventually, I began to read the poetry of famous authors. So, it will be through prose and poetry that I express my concern.

In *Libertarian Rants* I say harsh things about institutions and people who have profound cultural influence. This is not a criticism of free markets, wealth, or success. Far from it. Rather, it is a condemnation of the direction these folks seek to move Western culture toward.

You may say that my crude language is upsetting, that it detracts from my message. I would say that it expresses the anger of a significant percentage of Western society. Words are not violence. This is not a call for violence. If "upsetness" is your only takeaway, then you have missed the point. At the very least, consider the dire consequences of this divide should my perspective be accurate.

As a former communications professor, I maintain we need more and better communication, not speech codes and censure. I have great faith in the average citizen's ability to filter the information he or she encounters. Will *Libertarian Rants* influence culture in any manner? I hope so.

Warm-Up Rants

Abides the Bureaucrat · 4
Hate to Hear · 5
Free Market Flop · 6
No Shame · 8
Final Legs of Collectivism · 9
Boxers Lacking Balls · 10
Fragility · 11
Elephants and Donkeys · 12
Complacency's Fruit · 15
More Equal · 16
The Mad Haters · 18
Not-So-Great Expectations · 19

Abides the Bureaucrat

Overheard at DMV in Babylon: *"I'll need 15 copies, in cuneiform."*

Hate to Hear

We call it hate speech
lest our tenuous psyche splinter
sheltered, frail, puny

Free Market Flop

They say the free market isn't working
that we need a socialist solution
With greater government control
we'll achieve collective redistribution
Most applaud the government programs
our leaders push and promote
Why do we believe the propaganda
they shove down our throat

The vaunted New York Times
that esteemed bit of rag
Lauds big government programs
just freedom in a body bag
DC governs health insurance
even what light bulbs are okay
Regulates our college loans
mandates hourly rate of pay

It's said the free market isn't working
we must heed Michael Moore's concerns
With absolute government control
we could all feel the Bern
Regulation and intimidation
government agencies acting feral
Rules, fees, and bureaucrats
we're just luckless collateral

How the Free Market has fallen
the Au-Pair State arisen

Controls, promises, and subsidies
a market fenced, imprisoned
But free markets will never work
for people who won't grow up
When adolescence is the norm
adults sucking sippy cups

Would Hamilton and Madison
recognize our country today
They'd shake their heads
and proclaim they were betrayed
Time for a free-market revolution
the return of individual rights
Like Howard Roark in Fountainhead
let's set this republic aright

The lure of the nanny state
so enticing and addicting
Like Ulysses and the Sirens
it leads us to our doom
Who among us pulling at oars
can resist that honeyed song
The promise of love and rapture
of comfort, of life prolonged

The snare of the nanny state
get your beeswax at hand
Tie yourself to the mast
Ithaca ain't quite ready
The lure of the nanny state
so enticing and addicting
Like Ulysses and the Sirens
it leads us to our doom

No Shame

Rush for lowermost
tide of shame never rolls in
honor's a vapor

Final Legs of Collectivism
(hat tip to George Orwell)

Four legs good, two legs bad
Four legs good, two legs better
Two legs good, no legs – sad
Your legs good, our legs better
All legs are equal, but some legs
Are more equal than others

Boxers Lacking Balls

Caps without brains
shirts without chests
Boxers without balls
always the short game

What a charming story,
that Valley Forge
Lewis and Clark,
so dashing, so daring
Glass of red or white,
atop Normandy D-Day cliffs
Edmund Pettus Bridge,
well, bless their hearts

Throats without speech
feet without motion
Backs without spines
boxers without balls
Briefs or boxers
doesn't really matter
Cold, shrunken, withdrawn
cowardly hung

Courage deficit of the West
like boxers without balls
Revel in the past
just can't grow a pair

Fragility

The seasons of fear
built government dependence
our fragility

Elephants and Donkeys

Histories full of glory and guilt
few are heroes, know any names?
Villains too, of well-deserved repute
hundreds more just playing the game
They're Democrats and Republicans
creatures of the night
Sincerity they skillfully project
mouthpieces of selfishness and blight

The jackass and the pachyderm
feast on the public dime
Gorging at the DC trough
up the ladder they climb
Forget the Constitution
it's so old-fashioned
These urgent situations
require it be jettisoned

There is a zoo in Washington, DC
not where you expect it to be
Forget the Smithsonian National Zoo
on this reserve, animals make decrees
Take a trip to Independence and 1st
watch the swinish quench their thirst
Power and wealth they crave
their excuses well-rehearsed

You see, a Pachyderm is a loyal friend
he remembers those who feed him

No, he won't work for peanuts
fill his campaign trunk to the rim
Donkeys too are loyal friends
they know who butters their bread
Their greed requires they ignore us
obeying their paymasters instead

Since elephants and donkeys
are the elite of the nation
They take immense pride and pleasure
controlling for the duration
Take away freedom for safety's sake
the Bill of Rights must be retired
Liberty is overrated they say with a smile
no need for freedom, it's all prescribed

They take from Peter to pay Paul
redistribute with equity in mind
Winners chosen, losers too
coercion of labor is just fine
Like the emperors of Rome
they toss us stale bread
Like gladiators in the Coliseum
we're truly just walking dead

Two donkeys go into a bar
looking for goodies under the table
The corporatist opens his cookie jar
for their wives, a rare minx sable
He's big on family togetherness
so, cruise line tickets appear
Everyone does this in DC
just finished with an elephant ear

Loving the power of public domain
forget about individual property rights
Coerce and compel the landowner
change the zoning in dark of night
East and West Coast elite
brains, beauty, so well connected
The politician, journalist, corporatist,
power mashup of the perfected

Complacency's Fruit

Complacency's fruit
from tsunamis of success
the end of empire

More Equal

Pity the Deplorables stuck in the middle
we Brights must watch over them
God, guts, guns, so simplistic
it's the brave old world they seek
Fly-over country, why touch down
just unsophisticated freaks

All citizens are equal,
but some citizens are more equal than others
All property rights are equal,
but some property is more equal than others.
All speech is equal,
but some speech is more equal than others

Easily lead and easier driven
no critical thinking skills
Low IQ and lower breeding
NASCAR the biggest thrill
Bad habits and terrible teeth
RU486 the needed pill

All liberty is equal
but some liberty is more equal than others
All privacy is equal,
but some privacy is more equal than others
All business is equal,
but some business is more equal than others

High school diplomas a rare prize
carny careers, Walmart aspirations
Waffle House loyalty, Budweiser tastes
IQs lower than turkeys on the table
Working class, parochial, shallow
Clinton's basketful of Irredeemables

All genders are equal,
but some genders are more equal than others
All offenses are equal,
but some offenses are more equal than others.
All states are equal,
but some states are more equal than others

Individual sovereignty what a joke
they'll accept our offer
No need to double-think
twice the joy in harness
Success will be certain
just imagine the progress

All interest groups are equal
but some interest groups are more equal than others
All vocations are equal
but some vocations are more equal than others
All races are equal
but some races are more equal than others

All Americans are equal
but some are more equal than others
Inequality for the common good
crush their faces with our Armanis

The Mad Haters

Since it has some heft
what could it be besides hate
virtue demands so

Not-So-Great Expectations

Each one a victim
joyous low expectations
cesspool unity

Interlude – The Greeks Chime In

Socrates' Final Torment · 24
Dark Side of Plato · 25
Triggeripedes · 26
Wokememnon · 27
Antifacles · 28
Plato Steps in it Again · 29

Socrates' Final Torment

*"This hemlock is fair-trade, organic,
and patriarchy-free, right?"*

Dark Side of Plato

On class structure: *"I love me some ruling class elites scolding flyover country"*

Triggeripedes

Triggeripedes to the Oracle at Delphi:
*"You better have some phenomenal advice. I had to climb
at least 10 steps to get up this damn hill."*

Wokememnon

Come, Helen and Hector
Come, Hailey and Hunter
Join our regal struggle
We cancel the sure
Make love to the pure
Do it all with a chuckle

Antifacles

"Fascist violence must end. Where's my spear,
short sword, mask, and camera phone?"

Plato Steps in it Again

On the arts: *"My least favorite movie? Gattaca, of course!"*

Rants in the Main

Plants in the Rain

In Your Ears · 34
Coastal Despots · 35
Coup · 36
Eye of the Tiger · 37
The Supremes · 38
Lexington Green · 40
Vomit on My Door · 41
Her Question · 43
Hats Without Men · 45
Privacy Redux · 46
Star Spangled Inferno · 48
Pork Me · 50
Government Bitch · 53
Looking For an Endless Summer · · · · · · · · · · · · · · · · · 56

In Your Ears

"Speak, speak" lustfully roared the crowd
So, I gave it good, hard, and loud
My speech they called hateful
Cuz thinking is painful
Just tickling of ears allowed

Coastal Despots

The Beltway holds the richest counties
Westport, Connecticut, lives of ease
San Francisco Yacht Club all the rave
east coast elite riding the wave
West Coast elite, gated with hedges
power and wealth flow to the edges

East Coast patricians look down their noses
west coast elites with the finest clothes
Academia has lost its moorings
bureaucrats revel in fascist outpourings
Hollywood no more than a cocky bordello
the Media covers all with ink that's yellow

The Low Growth economy ain't makin it here
will inflation appear in our rearview mirror
Enough with printing money and public debt
record numbers underemployed, don't forget
Not lookin for redistribution of wealth
just want a job to care for myself

Once upon a time, I was self-reliant
now I'm just a government client
Uncle Sam my all-wise master
shields me from promised disaster
Strange, that those without need
demand that I bend the knee

Just a job to take care of myself

Coup

Left-wing views because you know what's true
Right-wing views seeing it's reason you pursue
No time for debate
Mulishness your trait
Conscience not open to a coup

Eye of the Tiger

Eye of the tiger
with urgency of a sloth
status quo secure

The Supremes

The Supremes now rule the land
As Congress has retreated
The Constitution their whipping boy
Creating laws as needed
Diana, Mary, and Florence
Knew this to be true
No mountain is high enough
To keep them off of you

It was 9 unelected men in black
Now women in black too
Doesn't really matter
Once they get through
If the Constitution doesn't address it
The urgency still requires it
Can't wait for the process to work
Cuz Congress might not resolve it

The Supremes, what a perfect title
Their brilliance we acknowledge
The brightest, not just rank in file
From only the best colleges
The third branch is afraid and weak
Their efforts so very timid
Yep, Congress just stays meek
Blame what someone else did

The Constitution a living document
So, squeeze it till it bleeds

Disregard the legal question
Focus on what you need
The opportunity a crisis gives
Cannot be neglected
Use it to achieve what's best
Compassion must be projected

We're calling you out US Congress
Pick up the mantle, stand up for us
Have some guts for once in your life
We expect you to make a fuss
Thanks to separated powers
You know us the best
Not the nine folks in black
Move, act, we'll pass the test

Some prefer the Supreme Court
Some prefer the supreme burrito
I prefer the House and Senate

Some prefer a supreme leader
Some prefer the supreme taco
I prefer the US Congress

Lexington Green

April green of Lexington
Animals graze, children play
It was early, dark, beneath the heavens
Last look at the North Star that day

The scarlet might of Britain filled their eyes
Just common men, no praetorian guard
With fields to tend, cows need milking
Dreaded bayonets, there the graveyard

A principle rooted them to that soil
With wood to chop, roofs to repair
Birthing a nation not the plan
No assurance what fruit might bear

Shots heard 'round the world
Merely the resolve of ordinary men
Bullets and bayonets tearing flesh
Buckman Tavern missing dear friends

Surely, they loved their lives
Plans for the future deep inside
Much to do this Wednesday morn
Yet they stood, stood, and died

April green out your front door
Tyranny now with new labels
Will the spirit of Lexington awaken
Or individual sovereignty be resigned to fable

Vomit on My Door

New York and DC,
jaws compelled to roar
LA spews the same vomit
on my front door
Puffery their power
pummel us by the hour with
*"Open your minds,
we'll hurl in some more"*

As brackish water needs filtration
media protects from disinformation
Pedigree married to clout
refinement deep up the snout
Thankfully focused on our salvation
like rabid feral hogs caught in rusty snares
Deplorables thrash about,
their rescue impair

*"Shut your pie holes, flyover folk
we know best cuz you ain't woke
Follow our directions
and you might have a prayer"*

What's a boorish country bumpkin to do?
Should we just lay down
while they run us through?
Our minds reject the puke they chuck
all we hear is cluck, cluck, cluck
We're not impressed by this elite crew

Arguments from authority,
just wobbly scree
While common sense and reasoning are free
take Stanford, Columbia, and NYU
The Ivy League and who knows who
credibility is earned,
So fuck your degree

Her Question

He caught my ear that night
Sure, he was good looking
It was the laugh that drew me
From far across the room
Just who was this guy
The one not drinking
He seemed to be relaxed
And didn't need attention

I'm not easy to please
Few men meet my standards
My list is long and explicit
But one question matters most
And if he measures up
We might just have a future

So, does he have a 401K
What's his debt load
Does he have a criminal record
Is he free from STDs
Does he live with his parents
Is life more than online gaming
A full-time job is required
Drug abuse a nonstarter

Everything lined up
He checked every box
But one question remained
Would he pass the test

He seemed so perfect
And my standards are high
My emotions fought against me
But I knew what must be said

I'm not easy to please
Few men meet my standards
My list is long and explicit
But one question matters most
If he measures up
We might just have a future

I held my breath, then blurted it out
"Are you a Libertarian?
That is: Do you value property rights
Is freedom of speech your idol
Limited governance your preference
And nonaggression a virtue
Are individual rights a given
Freedom from coercion a must
Free markets your passion
And all subsidies a curse?"

I'm not easy to please
Few men meet my standards
My list is long and explicit
But one question matters most

Hats Without Men

There was a dullard from Finance
who could not bring himself to dance
His ankles might turn out weak
so, he kept his prospects bleak
Safety became his only romance

Coffee shops filled with caffeine and the Quiet
like Easter Island heads living non-meat diets
Why, one could offend
or seem to defend
Soften your keystrokes, don't start a riot

Hats empty of courageous men
long, long, gone the Minutemen
Chests longing for a chance
only find safety dance
Maintain silence, mumble amen

Privacy Redux

Thank God for the IRS,
protecting us from dangerous folk
Our minds can't handle controversy,
it's for our good
The NSA has your back,
protecting you from the wicked
They've tapped your phone, your laptop,
as they should

J Edgar would be proud,
the FBI is back
Drones, snooping, recording,
we're grateful, in fact
Camera on my pc,
data mining, social media
They're busy hugging me,
how dare I suggest that's wack

We slept while safety crushed liberty,
and security replaced freedom
They even used a national crisis,
to further their control of us
In the name of promised certainty,
we gave up autonomy
The pursuit of happiness consumes us,
as life and liberty leave us

Oh, say can you see,
by the dawns early light

Any resemblance of the founders'
intentions for our life
Will the twilight's last gleaming
be the end of the experiment
Will our hard-earned freedom,
survive this perilous strife

If freedom means I take more risk,
I accept the consequences
I'd rather face terrorists,
than bureaucrats' decrees

Listen up you politicians,
listen up you judges
Read up on the Bill of Rights,
and set this people free
Oh, say can you see
what we once proudly hailed
A people chiefly self-governed,
as Jefferson hoped we would be

By the dawn's early light,
and twilight's last gleaming
I dream of individual rights,
returning to you and me

Star Spangled Inferno

It seems you're quite unhappy
Things ain't as they ought
So light up the stars and stripes
Burn our pride and delight

I hate to see our flag aflame
The smoke in my neighbor's eyes
A military veteran deeply seared
With wounds you cannot cauterize

It's just a piece of cloth
Some blue, some red, some white
A bunch of stripes, and some stars
Not a talisman in the wind

I squeeze my tired eyes
As the flames swallow
Cover my nose, the offense
Smells of cheap ignorance

You claim that it's your right
Yes, I certainly agree
But while you smolder
Old Glory warms my soul

Better to live where flags can burn
Live with the sorrow and anger
Than live where it's not allowed
Couldn't bear to live there

Go ahead and pierce my heart
Set Old Glory ablaze
In those flames, liberty comforts me
Your fury ignites my pride

Pork Me

Bacon, bacon, bacon
Who's got enough bacon?
Sizzle, sizzle, sizzle
Get me some DC bacon
Bacon, bacon, bacon
I like it smoked and cured
Sizzle, sizzle, sizzle
More bacon, more secure

We scream for budget cuts
The national debt a crime
Eager to slash another's pork
As long as it doesn't affect mine
Make my constituents happy
Add pork to a crucial bill
Butcher any courageous politician
Then dropkick him down the Hill

The aroma of bacon is irresistible
The attraction quite primal
Subsidies to corporations
And farmers gone viral
Tax breaks for non-profits
The military can't be pruned
Government is swelling
Entitlements have ballooned

Bacon, bacon, bacon
Who's got enough bacon?

Sizzle, sizzle, sizzle
Get me some DC bacon
Bacon, bacon, bacon
I like it smoked and cured
Sizzle, sizzle, sizzle
More bacon, more secure

The collective language of bacon
Is spoken across the nation
Individuals and corporations
Never need a translation
In bacon we do trust
Cuz bacon is so yummy
Glad to smooth our edges
Like big hugs from Mummy

Bacon clogs the arteries
Of the economic free market
Builds up the cholesterol
The national deficit our casket
Bacon makes us zombies
All we crave is pig meat
Government fires up the grill
We stagger to the mercy seat

Bacon, bacon, bacon
Who's got enough bacon?
Sizzle, sizzle, sizzle
Get me some DC bacon
Bacon, bacon, bacon
I like it smoked and cured
Sizzle, sizzle, sizzle
More bacon, more secure

Blame the politicians
Blame the lobbyists
Blame the system
Blame the courts

Blame the Man
Blame Jim Gaffigan
Blame everything but
What the mirror shouts

Government Bitch

I am dangerous
I am the mistake
I need control
I am a government bitch

The leash is uncomfortable
But risk far worse
Chance is unpredictable
Big Brother so certain

Liberty is over-rated
Safety all-consuming
Give the elite compliance
Like a government bitch should

I am dangerous
I am the mistake
I need control
I am a government bitch

We trust our master
The world's so complex
No man is an island
Big Brother knows what's best
From the cradle to grave
How could we survive alone
We rely on master's wisdom
Like a government bitch should

I am dangerous
I am the mistake
I need control
I am a government bitch

The world is so evil
We need to be protected
We cannot guard ourselves
Big Brother's the solution
We cannot think for ourselves
He knows our limitations
We have faith in the Master
Like a government bitch should

I am dangerous
I have made mistakes
Maybe I don't need control
I hate being a government bitch

I can be dangerous
I know I make mistakes
And the world is uncertain
There are no guarantees
Chance is so scary
So much can happen
But I can handle it,
don't worry

Freedom is dangerous
Make no mistake
But liberty means less control,
and no more government bitches
I don't need a Big Brother
Mine is doing just fine

My mind can handle the complex
The uncertain and the sublime

My limitations don't scare me
My heart is full of courage
Life was never meant to be
An eighty-year guarantee
No more government addicts
No more government whores
No more mainlining DC
No more government bitches

No more government dependency
No more government eunuchs
No more DC coercion
No more government bitches

Looking For an Endless Summer

Chase endless summer
craving happiness supreme
winter comeuppance

Interlude – Twisted Nursery Rhymes

Humpty Becomes Dumpty ·60
Fun with Jack n Jill · 61
Debtor's Nursery Rhyme · 62
Beltway Smudgery ·64
Lil Jack Cornered · 65
Chrometophobia ·66
Victim-Medes· 67

Humpty Becomes Dumpty

Humpty Lumpty sat on a wall
Peeling onions in search of it all
He never found meaning in the red
Sadly, the white was empty as his head

Jumpty off the wall Humpty
Idleness makes one grumpty
Yes, your landing might be bumpty
But responsibility will make you pumpty

But alas, poor Humpty
Wouldn't get off his rumpty
Was obsessed with bliss
Leaned over the abyss
Fell off like a chumpty
And so became Dumpty

Fun with Jack n Jill

Jack and Jill
Sought ecstasies and chills
Aimed for fun in the sun
Jack grew dull
Never felt full
Jill swallowed a gun

Debtor's Nursery Rhyme

One potato, two potato
Thirty plus trillion the sum
Our national debt keeps rising
More, more, more

Eeny, meeny, miny, moe
Federal spending out of control
Can't cut anything
No, no, no

Three blind mice
Plus 435 more
US House of Reps doing nothin
Won't, won't, won't

Twinkle, twinkle, little star
Federal Reserve's printing money
The Elite are fat and happy
Print, print, print

Now I lay me down to sleep
My earning power sinking deep
The dollar's value in a spin
Down, down, down

Jack be nimble, Jack be quick
Cowardly politicians in DC
Doesn't matter by what label
Same, same, same

Hickory, dickory, dock
The time is running out
Our debt will one day crush us
Pain, pain, pain

Mary had a little lamb
Government bribes us all
The budget must be cut
Slash, slash, slash

Michael rowed the boat ashore
No subsidy was needed
We know the cuts will hurt
Agreed, agreed, agreed

Little boy blue, blow that horn
Awaken the sleepy public
It's all your fault and all mine
Listen, listen, listen

Do you know the Muffin Man
Do you know your senator
Tell 'em you're an adult
Call, call, call

Not what your country can do for you
What you can do for your country
For our children's sake and liberty
Grow up, consider well, speak up

Beltway Smudgery

Jack and Jill
Went to Capitol Hill
To intern for a US senator
Jack came back
His soul covered in plaque
Jill with pockets full of mirrors

Lil Jack Cornered

Lil Jack Horner
Wept in the corner
Betrayed by virtuous friends
Her pronoun was he
Jack called him she
Doxed and canceled his end

Chrometophobia

Woke Jack, woker Jill
They never pay the bill
Their non-profit work's too vital
Capitalism be damned
Until no funds are at hand
Suddenly, they're entitled

Victim-Medes

Oh Jack, oh Jill
You lost your will
In victimhood you decayed
Though Jill knew better
She cared much lesser
Jack gulped the same Kool-Aid

Rants For Change

Suck-Filled Lives · 72
If Only Tinder · 74
DC Resistance · 76
Speak to Learn · 79
Big-Boy Pants · 80
Noun Worth Seeking · 81
Churning · 83
Offend Me, Please · 84
Who Said That · 87
Deplorables on the Hook · 88
Free to Fail · 89
Zenith of Skepticism · 91
The School of Thinking Slowly · 93
Pledge No Allegiance · 95

Suck-Filled Lives

Never a butterfly
always the cocoon

Easy, so easy
just let it go
Like the rock
in curling
Someone other
can take care

Simple, so simple
aftermath be damned
Hit that light switch
nothing to see

Safe, so safe
culpability eschewed
No need for worry

Comfy chair snuggles
cuz taking a stand
Costs so much more
than vanilla cappuccino

Safe, simple, so easy
hate friction,
Love tranquility
do what assuages

Your emotional state
what else matters

Surely, disrespect
and dissatisfaction
Will follow you
all the days of your life
And you will dwell in your
self-loathing and bitterness
forever

Never a butterfly
always the cocoon

Cocoon life smothers
cocoon life sucks

If Only Tinder

Right swipe, left swipe
the choice is yours to make
Left swipe, right swipe
sure hope they're not fake
Great eyes, nice teeth
a rockin' hot body
Right swipe, left swipe
trust they're into naughty

Fooled me once, shame on you
but now the scam's viral
Government promises run eternal
the lies and bullshit just spiral
A Ponzi scheme of generosity
I feel compelled to swipe right
My desires and conditioning
welcome this precious delight

Oh, my sweet Tinder app
where honest opinion reigns
Why can't my government dealer
be so easy to contain
The Nanny State keeps pushing
a seductive meal of tripe
How many do you know that
think before they swipe

Swipe left
swipe goodbye
Swipe away dependence
swipe away the government's offers
Swipe its control from your life
swipe a well-deserved farewell
Swipe ain't interested

Swipe away the Au Pair State

DC Resistance

The District of Columbia,
where tyranny resides
Politicians yearn to control
your every breath
Their nameless friends,
those civil servants
Making DC a scourge
until your well-timed death

So normal this addiction,
call it DC dependence
Recognize the cords
of regulation and coercion
Can't you feel their grip,
smell their fear of freedom
DC has us by the throat,
detox the solution

They control school loans,
control how you flush
They control your lighting,
control where you smoke
They run the Senate,
they run the House
Unaccountable bureaucrats
holding your yoke

Eminent domain,
paper, or plastic
Masking for safety,
food labels to protect
Miles per gallon required,
Slurpees just so big
Leaving us only choices,
of what they deem correct

You didn't build that business,
can't do it on your own
To transform America,
is the politicians' plan
The government as savior,
therapist, and chaperone
Democrats and Republicans,
willing to take a hand

Peace, security,
no, give me freedom
Forget safe spaces,
the risk is mine to take
Defy the gov't elite,
patience's not an option
Don't live in a stupor,
fight for what's at stake

DC resistance, Jefferson would be proud
DC resistance, shout it out loud
DC resistance, a patriotic cause
DC resistance, shout it out loud

Refuse DC, Reject DC,
resist, resist, resist

DC resistance, Jefferson would be proud
DC resistance, shout it to the crowds
DC resistance, the right thing to do

DC resistance, shout it out loud
renounce DC, rebuff DC
Resist

Speak to Learn

Sometimes I speak
and listening to my words
uncover my thoughts

Big-Boy Pants

I'm chief of buffoons
like all who plod on weary
big-boy pants await

Noun Worth Seeking

Perhaps it should be a verb,
as nouns seem so passive
Not so nice or kind,
happy as a burden
Unbound by compassion,
dreams or superstition
It demands more time,
no fan of comfort
Embraces all the risk,
has never met a victim

Maybe it should be a verb,
as nouns seem so stagnant
This would-be verb,
belongs to no political party
It has no allegiances,
loves logic and reason
Feelings must be panned,
despises hopes and wishes
Always relevant, never dated,
couldn't care less if hated

Conceivably, it could be a verb,
as nouns seem so fixed
Can't be bought,
keep the money in your pocket
No agenda beyond itself,
owned by no ism

Questions every single thing,
happy if proven wrong
When challenged by the fearful,
just laughs and marches on

Yes, let's label it a verb,
as nouns seem inactive
It calls on conscience,
relentless in pursuit
Will always seek more,
no satisfaction guarantees
Perhaps it should be a verb,
as nouns seem so static
The only belief I'll admit,
is trust in a noun called Truth

Churning

Waving the banner
Virtue quite sincere
Certain in allegiance
No shame in the mirror
And yet, something churns

Introspection bygone
Gather with those of same
The cataracts of Théoden
Your full inheritance
While within, something stirs

Alone at water's edge
Gazing at your image
Narcissus had nothing on you
So much to admire
A ripple, something churns

Must the heel of Achilles
Be your sworn enemy
What value vulnerability
Against a closed system
Chronic strain certain

Jeremiah had it wrong
The heart isn't all deceitful
Pacemaker be damned
The cures in mind
Churn baby, churn

Offend Me, Please

We used to protest against the Man
The powerful and wealthy
Now we use that same power
To control free speech and liberty
Cancel culture on the campus
Managed by Kent State's descendants
Flower power, fight the power
The new fascists know best

Diversity is a worthy pursuit
Tolerance a virtue
But when did freedom of speech
Become a threat to either
The 1960s were a crucial time
But the past is just a goodbye
Now those who gained the most
Are the architects of intolerance

Students demand safe spaces
Where nothing unwelcome is said
The violence of opposing ideas
Will crack their fragile psyche
What happened to the open campus
Where freedom of speech prevailed
And student voices protested
Against Johnson's and Nixon's war

Come on college professors
Step up school administrators
Remember your radical hippie days
And teach these children well
Feed them on the dreams you had
When McGovern was your hero
Help college students with the truth
You promoted in your tender years

You who are on the road
Remember it's a 2-way street
Perhaps this generation
Will call your words intolerant
You must keep the code you lived by
One that protects all free speech
The words of fools and charlatans
Will fail for the ideas they preach

The only safe space from words
Is found in the mind of the listener
Where experience and reason
Determine what rings true
Called the violence of words
Safe spaces are for cowards
Because the Marketplace of Ideas
Leads to mental resilience

Offend me please, offend me
Contest my ideas and beliefs
Make me a better person
Force me to deeply think
How will we ever mature

Unless our ideas are disputed
How to know they are compelling
Unless pressed to defend them

Offend me
Please, offend me

Who Said That

Eager to dispute
such abhorrent comments
Strangely, my stomach rumbled
a gnawing sense of discontent

My friends look bewildered
amygdala gripping my mind
Realization rumbling my belly
my words my core did malign

The ideas were adulterous
placing me opposite the barricade
Yes, yes, pride must yield to truth
but to mollify my angst, a crusade

Before me integrity and masquerade
live with the dissonance
Or face the conquest
and yield to conscience

Ahh....... Hello!

Deplorables on the Hook

Live right flyover folk
reject bitterness and wrath
be wise, act humbly

Free to Fail

Bailout the investment banker,
insure the farmer's crops
Cover the Big Apple,
the biggest airlines too
Savings and loan scandals,
Bear Stearns, and Freddie Mac
Everyone is too big to fail,
except for me and you

Big American auto companies,
protection without end
Take the money from everyone else,
taxpayers have no clue
Protect the licensed cab driver,
and the big banks too
Protect the Amtrak rail,
and Fannie when she's through

Build your house on the shore,
of an ocean that cannot be tamed
Government insures your home,
despite your acting dumb
Of all the ones that cannot fail,
government is the largest
It cannot fail nor shrink,
to accountability it's numb

When the masses are afraid,
government offers assurance
We give them power and control,
so freedom takes a beating
But fear of failure is good for business,
it keeps you sharp and alert
Worry stimulates needed change,
or success is usually fleeting

Here's to a level playing field,
where winning ain't predetermined
And success becomes the result,
of efforts each one makes
Thank God I'm free to fail,
yep, you heard me right
I don't need a guarantee,
of consequence-free mistakes

Free at last, free to fail
no more guarantees
Free to flourish or to crash
no more government nanny
Free at the first, free to the end
don't need no warranty
Free to pursue, free to gamble
content with uncertainty

Free at last, free to fail
no more guarantees
Free to flop or succeed
cover those government titties

Zenith of Skepticism

We prize trust,
honesty, and loyalty
throw in integrity and constraint
and why not, humility, too

Ascend skepticism,
broaden your vision,
claim your throne

Brought up to be virtuous,
expecting the same of
our leaders

Elitist bastards,
remember what honor is
and respect
the rule of law
and individual agency

Sure, consider us
the proletariat
plebians, serfs

Distrust you've fully earned,
aristocratic snobbery,
power corrupting absolutely

Hesitant citizen,
pull aside the veil,
verify, then trust
respect no longer a gimme,
high regard is earned
they smell of septic tank sludge,
our contempt has no end

A new virtue we declare,
skepticism to the fore
the zenith does so long,
Pyrrhon arise

Skeptical at the start,
skeptical to the end
Prove us wrong

The School of Thinking Slowly

Glory belongs to the immediate
Accolades to the swift
Of course, reward the first to post
Always the possibilities for grift

Quick on your feet is a blessing
As a runaway truck bears down
But little of life is as pressing
Time aplenty for another go-round

Thinking deeply requires patience
Hardly a virtue in a frenetic age
Yet the reward is securing truth
Unbridled curiosity engaged

Constraint is a gem oft-ignored
Perseverance a diamond in the making
Reach for dark full-bodied wine
Insights harvested for the taking

Fear and guilt twisting your gut
Read those who briskly oppose you
Grapple with nuance and complexity
Layers of insight you will accrue

Even impulse can be coached
Invest the time, slow it down
The School of Thinking Slowly awaits
Open enrollment in your hometown

The

School

of

Thinking

Slowly

Pledge No Allegiance

Seek truth
with reason your guide
Your conscience
for no allegiance set aside

Acknowledgment

Though standing on the shoulders of giants themselves,
these men are titans to me. We see further because of
Richard Dawkins, Milton Friedman, Sam Harris,
Rand Paul, and Steven Pinker.

Lastly, to no person am I more indebted than the late
Christopher Hitchens, who demonstrated the inviolate virtue
of skepticism, and the potency of sarcasm, yet never
succumbed to unremitting cynicism. His confidence
in human progress was matched by a playfulness
that made his commentary more palatable.

About the Author

Michael Schulte, writer and teacher, was raised in Detroit. The third of seven children. Michael attended a Catholic elementary school before completing his education in the public school system.

Debating prominent issues was routine in the Schulte household and heated exchanges were common. Since his adolescence, Michael married, earned two advanced degrees, had five children, and experienced the joy of being a grandfather ten times over.